BRAZIL
INSIGHTS

Special Dedication

To my friends Susan and Chris, please, join me in taking this memorable journey through Brazil: a colorful, rich, historic, stunning, serene, and vast South American Country.

Contents

Quick Facts Bout Brazil

The name 'Brazil' is borrowed from *'brazil wood';* a tree which anciently grew along the country's Coast. Notably, Brazil is the largest country in South America and the Fifth (5th) largest country in the world after Russia, Canada, United States, and China.

Brazil was a colony of Portugal, from early 1500 until the year 1822 when the country eventually secured its independence. Portuguese is the official language of Brazil. In the whole country, there are no regional dialects except for the languages spoken by a group of Indian tribes living within the country's remote reservations. Portuguese is the only recognized and widely spoken language in the day to-day lives of most Brazilians.

Brazil shares its borders with all countries in the South American region except for Chile and Ecuador. Specifically, countries which border Brazil are: Argentina, Bolivia, Colombia, French Guiana, Guyana, Paraguay, Peru, Suriname, Uruguay, and Venezuela. Unlike some of its neighboring countries, Brazil hasn't had any serious conflict or hostility with any of its neighbors. Brazilians are not only warm and welcoming; they also enjoy life to its available fullest, and most significant, value hard work, sports, and education.

Brazil is a Democratic Republic, with a Federal structure of Government, and devolved style of functioning. The country is strategically, divided into 26 States, and one Federal District, Brasilia, the country's capital. Each Brazilian State is autonomous; with respective Governors, Legislators, and Courts. The country's Municipalities are equally autonomous; with their own Mayors and Legislators. And to discharge the duties effectively, these Municipalities collect their own taxes.

According to the provisions of the country's Constitution, The President is both the Chief of State and Head of Government. He/She appoints the Cabinet; Ministers of State, to help in day-to-day running of the government. The country has a bicameral National Congress which is divided into: the Federal Senate, and the Chamber of Deputies.

Brazil has an estimated human population of over 210 million, with more than 75% living in the country's urban areas. A perfect example is exhibited in São Paulo; Brazil's largest and most populous City found in the southeast region of the country. Notably, São Paulo is the biggest and most populous city in the whole of South America.

Today, the most visited country in the continent of South America is Brazil. It is home to millions of animals and plant species; a unique biodiversity which is unrivaled by any other country in the world today.

Brazil experiences dominance of tropical climate. The second largest river after River Nile, the Amazon River, flows right through it. And as a result, over 60% of Amazon's rain forests are located in Brazil.

Brazil is a renowned agricultural hub, and the undisputed world's largest exporter of sugar, coffee, orange juice, soya, beef, tobacco and chicken. The Financial Times once described Brazil as *"a powerhouse whose size and efficiency few competitors can match"*.

Did You Know?

Brazil is the largest Portuguese- speaking country in the world. Portuguese speaking people are also referred to as Lusophones. Brazil is also the only Portuguese-Speaking Country in South America.

Brazil is a home to world's second biggest black population after Nigeria. And remarkably, it is also home to the largest number of people of Japanese ancestry outside native Japan. And more interestingly, more people of Lebanese or Syrian origin are found in Brazil in numbers bigger than the combined populations of Lebanon and Syria.

The most celebrated event in Brazil's calendar is the Carnival. This unique Brazilian celebration usually attracts millions of Brazilians and foreigners into Brazil's cities and Sambadromes; specially built settings where the carnival celebrations are held. No other country in the world organizes, or celebrates carnival the way Brazilians do. Carnival celebration is part and parcel of Brazil's culture, and they give it their all. Notably, the annual Carnival celebration in Rio de Janeiro is usually regarded as the world's biggest street party, attracting more than 2.5million people; both locals and foreigners).

Brazil has the world's largest Catholic population; at over 70% of its entire citizen population.
Brazil has one of the biggest economies in the world, in terms of gross domestic product (GDP) calculated from purchasing power parity (PPP). Many of its citizens have high buying power.

The capital city of Brazil is called Brasilia, while its largest city is São Paulo. Unlike most cities around the world, Brazil's most populous city, São Paulo, isn't the country's capital city.

Down Memory Lane: Brazil From 1500 To 2014

Brazil has a rich history stretching down to prehistoric times. Below are the time frames with respective highlights of some of the most important milestones in the history of Brazil.

1500 – 1654: 1500 represents the historic year when the Portuguese arrived in Brazil under the command of Pedro Alvares. Around 1630, the Dutch had started to invade parts of Brazil, but come the year 1654, they were fiercely driven away by the Portuguese; who once again, took control of the entire Brazilian territory.

1750 – 1821: Around 1750, Portugal signed a noteworthy treaty with Spain; to guarantee its rightful areas of rule within South America. Between the years 1808 to 1821, the Portuguese royals identified and relocated to Brazil's Rio de Janeiro, as their new capital and new focal center for operations. Rio was strategically positioned to allow them effectively manage their territories in Brazil and in Portugal.

1822 - 1889: Brazil attained its independence in the year 1822, and come the year 1888, the country successfully, abolished slavery. Then in the triumphant and historic year of 1889, Brazil was declared a Republic.

1917-1958: The year 1917 saw Brazil declare war on Germany, during the 1st World war. And in the year 1930, Getulio Vargas was elected by Brazilian Military Officials, to take charge of the country as a President.

In 1942, during the Second World War, Brazil declared war on the Axis. And the year 1945 witnessed the overthrowing of President Getulio Vargas, through a military coup; after being in power for more than 14 years. Then in the year 1945, Brazil became one of the founding members of United Nations Organization.

In the year 1946, Brazil adopted a new constitution, which gave more rights to its citizens. And come the year 1958, the country achieved a landmark world accolade; for the first time in their football sports history. The Brazilian football team was crowned champions in a FIFA World Cup tournament, after defeating Sweden 5-2 in an entertaining final match played in Sweden.

1960: This was a very emotional and a landmark year for the residents of Rio de Janeiro; as they witnessed Brazil transfer its capital from Rio de Janeiro to Brasilia. The real Cariocas (people born in Rio or people from Rio), who are still alive today haven't forgotten this fateful year. The events of 1960 remain an indelible stain in their memories.

1962-1992: For a record second time, the year 1962 saw Brazil crowned as champions in FIFA World Cup tournament; after defeating Czechoslovakia 3 – 1 in a match played in Chile's Estadio Nacional Julio Martínez Prádanos.

In the year 1964, the country's Military once more, took control of the Government. However, they would later return the government's control back to Civilian rule in 1985. But before then, the year 1970 again witnessed the country's football team crowned as World Cup Champions, for a record third time.

Then in the Year 1989, Fernando Collor de Mello was elected President, under direct elections. And in 1992, Rio de Janeiro achieved a landmark feat when it played host, for the first time, to more than one hundred World Leaders during an International World Summit Day.

1994-2014: The year 1994 saw Brazilian football team clinch the prestigious FIFA World Cup trophy, for a record 4th time, in a hotly contested World Cup final. Brazil beat Italy 3–2 in a post match penalty decider. And in the subsequent year of 1995, Fernando Henrique was elected Brazil's president.

Again, in 2002, Brazil, for another record 5th time, was crowned as world champions in FIFA World Cup tournament held in the Asian countries of South Korea and Japan. Brazil clinched the title after defeating their arch football rivals; Germany 2-0.

In the following year; 2003, Luiz Lula de Silva was elected the country's President, and afterwards ruled for two terms of 4 years a term. Then come the year 2011, Dilma Rousseff was elected as Brazil's first woman President. And in 2014, Brazil played host to the prestigious FIFA World Cup tournament.

Language

Portuguese is the official National language of Brazil. Nearly the entire Brazilian population can comfortably speak in Portuguese. A few exceptions are found among a minority group of Indian immigrants, whose main languages are: *Tupí, Arawak, Carib, and Gê.*

Brazil is the largest Portuguese- speaking country in the world. Also, it is the only Portuguese-Speaking Country in the whole of South America. Remarkably, Brazilians speak Portuguese with no or very few cases of regional dialects!

Other languages which commonly feature in most Brazilian Cities include: German, English, French, Italian, and Spanish. In fact, foreign languages are often taught in a number of Brazil's learning institutions, and in private lessons.

Significantly, most Brazilians can comfortably communicate in Spanish, but they prefer to communicate in Portuguese.

Some Common Portuguese Words/Phrases

When in Brazil, the best language to use in speaking to the locals is Portuguese. Some locals understand Spanish, but they do not like to speak or to be engaged in Spanish.

In case of any communication barrier, it is advisable to write down your destination, and show it to your guide, or to the other party. This is mostly common when making inquiries.

Below are some of the common words/phrases/sentences/ that may help any visitor in Brazil, to easily connect with the locals.

Greetings

Hello - *Olá!*
Hello! How are you? -*Olá! Como vai?*
Hi - *Oi*
Nice to meet you - *Prazer em conhecê-lo.*
Welcome! (greetings) - *Bem-vindo (male)/ bem-vinda! (female).*
Thank you very much - *Muito obrigado (men)/ Muito obrigada! (female).*
I'm fine, thanks! - *Bem, obrigado! (men)/ Bem, obrigada! (female).*
Hey Friend - *Ei, amigo(male)/ amiga(female).*
I'm fine - *Eu estou bem.*
Good Morning - *Bom dia.*
Good Afternoon - *Boa tarde.*
Good Evening - *Boa noite.*
Good Night - *Boa noite.*
See you later! - *A gente se vê mais tarde!*
Goodbye - *Adeus.*

Seeking for help or asking questions

I need the police - *Chamar a polícia.*
I need a doctor - *Preciso de um medico.*
Come with me! - *Venha comigo!*
Can you help me? - *Você pode me ajudar?*
I am looking for Frank - *Estou procurando o Frank.*
Do you speak.."A"? - *Voce fala.."A"?*
Where is.."A"? - *Onde está"A"?*
Call the fire services - *Chamar os bombeiros*
What is your name? - *Qual é o seu nome?*
My name is 'X' - *Meu nome é 'X'*
Where do you live? - *Onde você mora?*
Excuse me (to ask for something) - *Por favor*
Excuse me (permission to pass) - *Com licença.*
Where do you live? - *Onde você mora?*
Do you speak English? - *Você fala Inglês?*
Does anyone here speak English - Alguém aqui fala Inglês?

You are very kind! - *Voce é muito gentil?*
What do you do for a living? - *Com que você trabalha?*
What time is it? - *Que horas são?*
Can you speak slowly? - *Pode repetir devagar, por favor?*
How much? - *Quanto?*

In case of emergency

I have had a car accident - *Eu sofri um acidente de carro*
Where is the nearest hospital? - *Onde é o hospital mais próximo?*
I have an accident - *Eu sofri um acidente.*
Is there a pharmacy near here?: *Há uma farmácia aqui perto?*
I need an ambulance - *Preciso de uma ambulância.*
I have been robbed /mugged - *Eu fui vitimo de um assalto* or *Eu fui roubado.*
This is an emergency - *Temos uma emergência.*

Encouragements

Congratulations! - *Parabéns!*
Good luck! – *Boa Sorte!*
Don't worry! - *Não se preocupe!*

General

I don't understand - *Eu não entendo.*
Please: - *Por Favor*
Yes – *Sim.*
No – *Não.*
No Problem! - *Não tem problema!*
I don't know! - *Não sei!*
Sorry! (For a mistake) - *Desculpe!*
Enjoy your meal! - *Bom apetite!*
Big/ Small - *Grande/ Pequeno.*
I'm hungry/ thirsty - *Estou com fome/ com sede.*
Very Sick - *Muito doente.*

Exclamations

Really! - *É mesmo?*
Look! - *Veja!*
What? /Where? - *O que?/ Onde?*
Oh! That's good! - *Oh! Que bom!*

Counting numbers

One, Two, Three, Four, Five - *Um, Dois, Três, Quatro, Cinco.*
Six, Seven, Eight, Nine, Ten - *Seis, Sete , Oito, Nove, Dez.*

Culture

The Brazilian culture is extraordinarily rich as a result of a mixture of many nationalities from different countries, with different backgrounds and different cultures.

Ranging from the Portuguese, to native Indians, and finally to an influx of African slaves, the country has over the years absorbed divergent set of cultures which also encompasses different food and musical varieties.

The Brazilian rich culture is best exhibited in their: food, religion, dance styles, singing styles, sports, and other activities.

Preserved exhibitions are usually found in the country's major tourist attraction areas such as the local beaches, museums, Sambadromes; during carnival celebrations, and even in residential places.

Religion

Brazil's Constitution guarantees absolute freedom of worship to all its Citizens. Notably, Roman Catholics are the majority, with a significant continued growth in numbers of Protestant groups.

Some Brazilians are members of Independent Pentecostal Churches, while others are adherents of Candomblé; a religion believed to have been brought into Brazil by the Yoruba slaves from both Benin and Nigeria.

Followers of mainstream Protestant denominations from United States and Europe have equally grown in numbers. These mainstream Protestant denominations include: The Methodists, The Lutherans, The Baptists, and those adhering to Episcopalism. There are also members of the Church of Jesus Christ of Latter Day Saints (Mormons); a composition of small minorities of Jews, Moslems, and Buddhists.

There is another group of the Spirits or Kardecists; who strictly follow the doctrines of the late French Psychic researcher, Allan Kardec. (Allen Kardec believed in reincarnation, which is the center of belief in Spiritism or Kardecism).

Then, there are also members of the Muslim community. Islam in Brazil was first practiced by the early African slaves. They are believed to have led the earliest slave revolt in the country. According to IBGE Census of 2010, the number of people following Islam in Brazil was 35, 167.

Education System

The Brazilian Educational system consists of both Public (Federal, State and Municipal) and Private Institutions.

According to the provisions of the country's Constitution, education is regarded as compulsory to all persons aged 7 to 14 years. Significantly, the Federal Government (National Government) free offers public education. This enviable feat is made possible through the allocation of over 20% of the State and Local tax revenues towards education.

The Federal Government also offers appropriate interventions and financial subsidies to a number of poor families. This helps to effectively bar children from such disadvantaged backgrounds from falling into traps of child labor.

The Brazilian Education is managed by the Ministry of Education, with the Federal Council of Education playing the role of the Principal Standard-Setting Agency. On the other hand, the country's municipalities are responsible for enforcing education related regulations.

The School system starts from Pre-School, Elementary or First-Degree (*I Grau*), Secondary or Second-Degree (*II Grau*) to Secondary, University and all the way to Postgraduate Levels of study. Elementary Schools are designed to cover the basic general education essentials like learning Portuguese Language, Science, Mathematics, History, and Arts. In grade two, a secondary language like English is introduced.

From the elementary level, students then move to a three-year Secondary School level. Here, courses like Biology, Physics, Agriculture, Biology, are introduced. Students who gain qualifying marks for higher education then proceed to various universities in pursuit of relevant undergraduate degrees.

The normal duration for an undergraduate course is four years. However, there are certain courses like engineering or medicine which may take five to six years to complete.

Telephone Communications

The Brazilian telecommunications industry is effectively regulated by *Agência Nacional de Telecomunicações,* (The National Telecommunications Agency) popularly shortened as ANATEL. Notably, ANATEL has already introduced phone number portability in the country.

Public telephones can be accessed easily all over. However, they do not take coins. You need to buy a phone card from nearby shops, dealers, malls, and supermarkets. The beauty of the phone cards is that they are available for purchase in various denominations, making them affordable the wider public.

Some of the phone technologies in Brazil include; GSM, TDMA, AMPS, CDMA, CDMA 2000 and WCDMA.

Brazil's international dialing code is **+55.**

For local phones, digits 2 to 5 are reserved for fixed lines, while digits 6 to 9 are reserved for mobile lines. If you were to make a call and the phone number has 2 to 5 digits, then that's a fixed line. And if it has 6 to 9 digits, then that's a mobile line. But mostly, a number of mobile phones have 8 or 9 digits.

Some of Brazil's phone companies include: Embratel, Brasil Telecom, Vivo, Tim, Claro, Oi, and Gvt.

Examples on how to make a phone call

Due to its vastness, for purposes of phone communications, the country is partitioned into different codes (area codes). These area codes are an allocation of two digits, and are geographically distributed across the country.

To call any number in any region within Brazil, you are required to first dial a '0' trunk prefix, followed by 'a phone carrier selection code', followed by 'the area code', and then the 'phone number' comes last.

The phone companies have each been allocated codes (phone carrier selection code). Some of these companies' phone carrier selection codes are: 12 CTBC, 14 Brasil Telecom, 15 Vivo, 21 Claro, 25 GVT, 31 Oi, and 41 TIM.

Example 1: To call a number say 33333333 in Fortaleza whose area code is 85, using a long-distance carrier say Oi whose selection code is 31, you will have to dial **0 31 85 33333333**. *(A '0' trunk prefix must be dialed before dialing the phone carrier selection code, followed by the area code, and then the phone's number).*

When making outbound calls (calls going outside Brazil), you must first dial a '00' trunk prefix, followed by the carrier selection code, the country's code, the country's region code, and then the phone number.

Example 2: To call a number say 1234567 in Washington DC (Area Code 202) in the USA (Country Code 1), using say TIM (Carrier code 41) as your preferred carrier, then you will have to dial: **00 41 1 202 1234567**. *(A '00' trunk prefix must be dialed before dialing the phone carrier selection code, followed by the country's code, the country's region code, and then the phone's number).*

Kindly note that whether you are using a mobile phone or a public phone, the procedure for calling any phone number is similar.

You can rent a cell phone from the local hotels, lodges, or restaurants at a fee. Also, you can use telephones installed inside your hotel room, but its usage will attract a further service charge fee on top of the normal bill you've incurred in making any call.

Emergency Telephone Numbers

In case of any emergent issue or scenario, below are some of the emergency numbers you can call in Brazil.

Ambulance: **192**

Fire Department: **193**

Military Police: **190**

Human Rights Secretariat: **100**

Federal Highway Police: **191**

Federal Police: **194**

Civil Police: **197**

State Highway Patrol: **198**

Civil Defense: **199**

The Government

Brazil is a Legal Democratic State, founded on *Sovereignty, Citizenship, Dignity of Human Persons, Social values of Labour and of Free Enterprise, and Political Pluralism.* According to the country's constitution, all power originates from the citizens, who exercise it by means of democratically elected representatives.

Brazil's Federal Government has three levels of powers, operating independently, and harmoniously, under a system of checks and balances.

Below are the three levels of power in Brazil:

- The Executive
- The Legislature
- The Judiciary.

The Executive

According to provisions of the Constitution, The President of the Republic; with the assistance of Ministers of State, is charged with the responsibility of exercising the country's executive power.

The President has the powers to appoint and dismiss Ministers of State. These Ministers are directly answerable to him. Any Minister of State can be summoned to appear before the Senate or any of its committees. Also, they can be summoned to appear before the Chamber of Deputies.

The President and the Vice President are elected on a four-year term. Nonetheless, the country's Constitution has provisions for impeaching the President through the Congress.

Should the Office of the President fall vacant, then Constitution provides for the Office of the Vice President to fill in; for the remainder of the original term. However, in the absence of the Vice President, the President of the Chamber of Deputies (Speaker of the House), would take charge. And, in the absence of President of the Chamber of Deputies, the President of the Senate would take charge. This line of succession eventually reaches the President of the Federal Supreme Court (Chief Justice).

The Legislature

The Legislative body of Brazil's Federal Government is known as the National Congress of Brazil (*Congresso Nacional do Brasil*).

The Congress is bicameral; consisting of the upper house and the lower house (The Federal Senate and The Chamber of Deputies).

The Federal Senate - *Senado do Brasil* (The Senate of Brazil) operates as the upper house of the National Congress of Brazil.

The Senate has 81 seats; three Senators from each of the 26 States, plus three Senators from the Federal District, who are elected on a popular vote for a term of 8 years. However, in every four years, renewal of either one third or two-thirds of the Senate, and of the delegations to States and Federal District usually takes place. These elections are spread out so that two-thirds of the upper house is up for election at one time and the remaining one-third four years later.

The Chamber of Deputies - The Chamber of Deputies is composed of 513 Federal Deputies, who are elected by relative representation of votes to serve a four-year-term.

Each State is eligible for a proportional allocation of seats, depending on their respective populations. (This usually ranges between 8 seats for the least populous state, to around 70 for the most populous state).

The Judiciary

The Brazilian Judicial powers are vested in the Supremo Tribunal Federal – STF (The Federal Supreme Court), in the Superior Tribunal de Justiça – STJ (Superior Court of Justice), in the Regional Courts, and in some specifically designed Courts for handling Military affairs, Labour affairs, Election affairs, and other important matters. The Judges and Justices for all these Courts; at State and Federal Levels, are usually permanently appointed (appointed for life).

The apex of Brazil's Judiciary is the Federal Supreme Court. Though it has its seat in Brasilia, it holds its jurisdiction throughout the country. It is composed of Justices of proven Legal and Constitutional Training and Experience, who are usually appointed by the President; after approval by the absolute majority of the Federal Senate.

The Country's Constitution

Brazil's Constitution was promulgated on the 5th of October, 1988, by a specially empowered National Congress.

Article three of the Constitution highlights the fundamental objectives of the Federative Republic of Brazil:

- *To guarantee National Development.*
- *To eradicate poverty and substandard living conditions, and to reduce social and regional inequalities.*
- *Build a free, just, and solidarity-based society.*
- *To promote well-being of all, without prejudice as to origin, race, sex, color, age, and any other forms of discrimination*

According to the Constitution, all persons are deemed equal before the law of the land, without any distinction whatsoever.

Any person living in Brazil; citizen or foreigner, is assured of the sacredness of his or her rights to: life, liberty, security, equality, and property.

The National Symbols

The Brazilian National symbols include:

- **The Coat of Arms.**
- **The National Flag.**
- **The National Anthem.**

The Coat Of Arms

Brazil's Coat of Arms is made up of five-pointed yellow-and-green stars enclosing a blue circle in the middle, and surrounded by tobacco, and coffee plants on the right-hand side and left-hand side respectively.

The middle blue circle represents the Southern Cross, and is beautifully covered by twenty seven (27) stars, representing the twenty six (26) states in Brazil plus the one (1) Federal District, Brasilia.

The coat of arms is also enclosed by a blue ribbon on its lower end with inscription of the words '*República Federativa do Brasil,* 15 de Novembro, de 1889'. (Federative Republic of Brazil, November 15, 1889).

The National Flag

The Brazilian National Flag is popularly referred to as *Bandeira do Brasil* in the Portuguese Language. It was originally designed by Raimundo Mendes, and was formally adopted in its original form as the Country's National Flag in the year 1889.

Other persons who are linked with coming up with the flag include; Manuel Pereira Reis, Miguel Lemos, and Décio Villares. The flag is an iconic decoration of three colors: green, yellow and dark blue. The green color represents Brazil's lush vegetation, while the yellow color is a representation of Brazil's wealth of gold. And the dark blue color represents the deep hue of the sky in country's tropics.

The flag is modeled out of three shapes: An outer green rectangular shape enclosing a yellowish diamond-like shape, and the yellowish diamond-like shape also encloses a blue colored circle with inscription of the words' *Ordem E Progresso'* from the left hand side to the right hand side. The English interpretation of the inscription is *'Order and Progress'*.

In the midst of the dark blue circle is a careful alignment of twenty seven (27) - five (5)-pointed stars, a representation of all the twenty six (26) states in Brazil plus the one (1) Federal District, Brasilia.

Use of The National Flag.

According to the provisions of the Brazilian Constitution, the following rules apply to the use of the National Flag:

- It must always be hoisted at the Praça dos Três Poderes in Brazil's capital city of Brasília. Equally, The Flag must be raised and lowered each day at the: Presidential Palaces, Diplomatic Missions or Consulates, compounds of Government Ministries, National Congress, Supreme Federal Tribunal, and Supreme Court of Justice, amongst other popular public and private places and Institutions.

- It must be hoisted at important National and regional events.

- If any other flag is to be hoisted alongside the Brazilian National Flag, that flag must be hoisted on the right hand side of the Brazilian flag, unless the Brazilian flag is in some foreign Mission. And significantly, the Brazilian

Flag must first reach the top of the flagpole, and also be the last to be lowered down

- Whenever a period of National Mourning is declared by the country's President, the flag must be carefully, hoisted at half-mast. This is usually, systematically, done by first hoisting it all the way to the top of the pole, then lowering it carefully to half of the pole.

- November 19Th is a day marked by Brazilians as a Flag Day. During this occasion, any Flag that is out of use; old or torn, is officially burnt at a military facility.

The National Anthem

The Brazilian National Anthem was composed by Francisco Manuel da Silva, and was formally adopted on 13th of April, 1922. 13th April is therefore, the *Day of the National Anthem*. The Brazilian National Anthem is called *Hino Nacional Brasileiro* in Portuguese.

Turn to the next page for the stanzas of the Brazilian National Anthem (in both English and Portuguese)

The first stanza of the National Anthem

In Portuguese	English Translation
First Stanza	**First Stanza**
Ouviram do Ipiranga as margens plácidas	The placid banks of Ipiranga heard
De um povo heroico o brado retumbante,	The blaring shout of a heroic folk
E o sol da Liberdade, em raios fúlgidos,	And the sun of Liberty in shining rays
Brilhou no céu da Pátria nesse instante.	Shone in homeland's sky at this instant.
Se o penhor dessa igualdade	If the pledge of this equality
Conseguimos conquistar com braço forte,	We could conquer with strong arm,
Em teu seio, ó Liberdade,	In thy bosom, O freedom,
Desafia o nosso peito a própria morte!	Our chest defy death itself!
Ó Pátria amada,	O beloved,
Idolatrada,	Idolized homeland,
Salve! Salve!	Hail, hail!
Brasil, um sonho intenso, um raio vívido,	Brazil, an intense dream, a vivid ray
De amor e de esperança à terra desce,	Of love and hope descends to earth
Se em teu formoso céu, risonho e límpido,	If in thy comely, smiling and limpid sky
A imagem do Cruzeiro resplandece.	The image of the (Southern) Cross blazes.
Gigante pela própria natureza,	Giant by thine own nature,
És belo, és forte, impávido colosso,	Thou art beautiful, thou art strong, an impavid colossus,
E o teu futuro espelha essa grandeza.	And thy future mirrors thy greatness.
Terra adorada	Adored Land
Entre outras mil	Amongst a thousand others
És tu, Brasil,	Art thou, Brazil,
Ó Pátria amada!	O beloved homeland!
Dos filhos deste solo	Of the sons of this ground
És mãe gentil,	Thou art kind mother,
Pátria amada,	Beloved homeland,
Brasil!	Brazil!

The second stanza of the National Anthem

Second Stanza

Deitado eternamente em berço
esplêndido,
Ao som do mar e à luz do céu
profundo,
Fulguras, ó Brasil, florão da América,
Iluminado ao sol do Novo Mundo!

Do que a terra mais garrida
Teus risonhos, lindos campos têm mais
flores,
"Nossos bosques têm mais vida",
"Nossa vida" no teu seio "mais
amores".

Ó Pátria amada,
Idolatrada,
Salve! Salve!

Brasil, de amor eterno seja símbolo
O lábaro que ostentas estrelado,
E diga o verde-louro dessa flâmula
- Paz no futuro e glória no passado.

Mas se ergues da justiça a clava forte,
Verás que um filho teu não foge à luta,
Nem teme, quem te adora, a própria
morte.

Terra adorada
Entre outras mil
És tu, Brasil,
Ó Pátria amada!

Dos filhos deste solo
És mãe gentil,
Pátria amada,
Brasil!

Second Stanza

Eternally lying down on splendid
cradle,
At the sound of the sea and the light of
the deep sky,
Thou flarest, O Brazil, crocket of
America,
Illuminated by the sun of New World!

Than the showiest land,
Thy smiling, pretty prairies have more
flowers
"Our grooves have more life",
"Our life" in thy bosom "more loves".

O beloved,
Idolized homeland,
Hail, hail!

Brazil, of eternal love be a symbol
The starred labarum which thou
displayst
And say the laurel-green of thy
pennant
'Peace in the future and glory in the
past.'

But if thou raisest the strong cludge of
Justice,
Thou wilt see that a son of thine
doesn't flee from battle,
Nor fears who loves thee by its own
death.

Beloved Land,
Amongst a thousand others
Art thou, Brazil,
O beloved homeland!

Of the sons of this ground
Thou art gentle mother,
Beloved homeland,
Brazil!

The Geographical Partition of Brazil

Brazil is geographically divided into five (5) major regions:

- **The Southeast Region.**
- **The Southern Region.**
- **The Northern Region.**
- **The Northeast Region**
- **The Centralwest Region.**

These regions are merely geographical and not political. They serve no administrative functions as they do not have any form of government. Nonetheless, these regions are highly regarded and are statistically used when it comes to allocation of developments funds by the Federal government.

Below are some of the highlights of Brazil's five major regions.

Southeast Region

The States found in this region include: Rio de Janeiro, São Paulo, Minas Gerais, and Espírito Santo.

It is a densely populated region with a concentration of valuable industries and therefore, unquestionably, reigns as the economic and industrial hub of Brazil. More specifically, Rio de Janeiro and São Paulo have since time memorial, been Brazil's hubs for commerce and manufacturing. Notably, São Paulo is still Brazil's commercial hub even to date.

This region has fertile agricultural land, and is equally endowed with minerals. It is known for the best production and processing of; coffee, grains, fresh and processed foodstuffs, all for local and international consumptions.

Southern Region

This region, just like the Southeast region, is equally developed. It however, has vast plains, which are locally known as the pampas. These pampas offer traditional grazing activities and have given rise to the *gaucho*, the famous Brazilian equivalent of the American cowboy.

One of the world's wonders, the Iguaçu Falls, located on the border between Brazil and Argentina is located towards the west of this region. Equally, Itaipu, the largest hydroelectric dam in the world is found in this region.

This region houses the states of: Paraná, Santa Catarina, and Rio Grande do Sul.

Northeast Region

This region is characterized by vast stretches of land and periodical drought occurrences.
It is home to over 25% of the Brazilian population and has a record number of oil fields; signifying its enviable economic potential to the country's economy.

The Brazilian Federal Government is working round the clock, through provision of relevant interventions and resources to ensure that this region rightfully, contribute meaningfully, towards the economic building of the country.

The states found in this region are: Maranhão, Piauí, Ceará, Rio Grande do Norte, Paraíba, Pernambuco, Bahia, Alagoas, and Sergipe.

Northern Region.

This region houses the Amazon basin. It is largely covered by abundant tropical rain forests, and is one of the regions with the largest concentration of fresh water in the world.

The states found in this region are: the Amazonas, Pará, Acre, Rondônia, Roraima, Amapá, and Tocantins.

Centralwest Region.

This region is widely covered with Savannas and Tropical Grasslands. Initially, this region was sparsely populated but has of late seen an upsurge in its population with an increase in the number of industries.

The Central West Region is home to the enviable Mato Grosso swamplands (Pantanal *Mato-grossense*), one of the Country's wildlife paradises. Brasilia, The Country's only Federal District is equally, located in this region.

The Federal Government has over the years, reserved large chunks of land in this region for the native Indian tribes, who were the ancestral occupants of this region.

States found in the Centralwest region of the country include: Mato Grosso, Mato Grosso do Sul, Goiás and the Distrito Federal.

States

The Federative Republic of Brazil is made up of twenty-six (26) States and one (1) Federal District (*distrito federal*), in which the Federal capital, Brasília, is found.

Initially, these States were classified as Provinces, until the year 1889, when they were officially converted into States.

Each Brazilian State has its own government, with a structure that reflects that of the Federal Government. However, these States have drafted and adopted certain legislations, which are not a reserve of the Federal Government.

A Governor is the Executive head of the State.

Governors are elected via direct popular vote. Each State equally, has a State Assembly which forms the Chamber for State Legislations. Then there is the State Judiciary, which operates in a Federal pattern, and has a defined jurisdiction; in order to avoid any conflict with the Federal Courts.

Below are the names of the twenty-six (26), Brazilian States plus the one (1) Federal District, and their corresponding capitals. The States are indicated in Bold with the corresponding capital city alongside.

List of Brazilian States with their capitals

No	Name of State	Capital
1	**Acre**	Rio Branco
2	**Alagoas**	Maceió
3	**Amapá**	Macapá
4	**Amazonas**	Manaus
5	**Bahia**	Salvador
6	**Ceará**	Fortaleza
7	**Distrito Federal**	Brasília

8	Espírito Santo	Vitória
9	Goiás	Goiânia
10	Maranhão	São Luís
11	Mato Grosso	Cuiabá
12	Mato Grosso do Sul	Campo Grande
13	Minas Gerais	Belo Horizonte
14	Paraná	Curitiba
15	Paraíba	João Pessoa
16	Pará	Belém
17	Pernambuco	Recife
18	Piauí	Teresina
19	Rio de Janeiro	Rio de Janeiro
20	Rio Grande do Norte	Natal
21	Rio Grande do Sul	Porto Alegre
22	Rondônia	Porto Velho
23	Roraima	Boa Vista
24	Sergipe	Aracaju
25	Santa Catarina	Florianópolis
26	São Paulo	São Paulo
27	Tocantins	Palmas

N/B: *Rio de Janeiro and São Paulo are the two famous Brazilian States whose capitals have names identical to State names.*

Cities

Brazil has a record number of cities in each of its twenty six (26) States plus the one (1) Federal District.

These cities are always packed by locals and visitors; because of the rich Brazilian cultures, colors, and flavors, that have a perfect exhibition within them. It is estimated that more than 75% of Brazilians live in the cities.

Below are highlights of some of Brazil's major and favorite cities:

Brasília

Brasília is a Federal District and has been the country's capital city since the year 1960. It is a city which was built from scratch, and is well-known for its awesome planning which is accredited to the late Oscar Niemeyer and Lucio Costa. It took the country only four years to have Brasilia built.

'Brasilia is in the shape of a bent bow and arrow or an airplane when viewed from the skies; and is very rationally, divided into regions and quadrants that all have their designated purposes: specific areas for residential houses, allocated areas for hotels, space for commercial areas, etc. Aesthetically, the view is quite remarkable from the top, and as a plan on papers it looks great.'….. {*www.braziltravelinformation.com*}.

Due to its remarkable architectural designs, coupled with lots of greenish environs, Brasilia is classified by UNESCO as a world heritage site. Brasilia offers a vital link between East and West, North and South of South America.

Salvador

Salvador is a City found in Bahia State. Salvador was the first capital of Brazil, and is currently the capital of the state of Bahia.

It is believed that Salvador was founded by the Portuguese around the year 1549, to act as a stop for their ships. It is a colorful, musical and a city rich in historical value. Salvador equally, has over 30 miles of beautiful beaches and well cared ecological sites, making it one of the most popular destinations in Brazil.

Salvador has a busy port along the Atlantic Ocean, and the City is populated with old buildings of churches, which colorfully, decorate its streets and environs. Salvador is home to a large family of Afro-Brazilian community and is famous for the *Candomblé;* a religion inherited from ancient Yoruba slaves from Nigeria and Benin.

"European, African and American heritages have been intricately woven together in Salvador. There, three cultures anciently, interacted and were transformed by the shared climate, geography, and social history. As a result, something entirely new has emerged. Salvador is culturally vital and defiantly different: a melting pot instead of a mosaic; a soup instead of a salad." ….. {*www.bahiatursa.ba.gov.br*}

Salvador is also famous for its well organized Street Carnival Celebrations; where many inhabitants fill the streets, annually, to dance to sounds of music and express their happiness.

Rio de Janeiro

Rio de Janeiro hosted Brazil's capital city before being relocated to Brasília, the current capital city.

Popularly known as 'The Brazilian City that never sleeps,' Rio de Janeiro is Brazil's most famous City and is every tourist's dream destination.

Rio is endowed with incomparable and naturally; rich beauty, rich history, and most of all, an enviable and transmittable joy of the *Cariocas*– people from Rio de Janeiro.

The urban buildings in Rio de Janeiro are marvelously nestled between glorious bays and stunning beaches on one side, and rising mountainous range, covered by a lavish tropical forest on the other side. Some of Rio's stunning beaches include: Ipanema, Copacabana, and Leblon. Rio's New Year Party celebration is an unforgettable, lovely, experience.

Rio de Janeiro is also famous for the manner in which Carnival celebrations are organized. Carnival celebration in Rio is regarded as "the world's largest street party" in which thousands of people get involved and they go to the "Sambódromo"; a specially built facility to host the Carnival.

Some of Rio's beauties are highlighted in the country's postcards: the Sugarloaf Mountain, and the enviable Corcovado Mountain where Christ the Redeemer statue elegantly stand.

São Paulo

São Paulo is Brazil's largest and most populated city. It is the largest city in the whole of Latin America.

With a population of over 11 Million inhabitants, São Paulo offers a wide variety of cultural diversions and endless cooking variety, with more than 14,000 hotels and restaurants.

São Paulo is capital of a State with a similar name; São Paulo. It is a commercial and financial hub of Brazil.

It is one of the most popular Cities frequented by tourists due to availability of abundant green parks and spectacular landscapes.

Fortaleza

Fortaleza is the capital of Ceará State. It is one of the oldest Brazilian Cities, dating back to the 1600's. Situated in the northeast region of the country, the city has a growing population, which is currently an average of over 2.6 million people,

Fortaleza is popular for a bustling nightlife, and stunning and blissful several kilometers of beaches.

Some of Fortaleza's attractions include: Fortaleza Cathedral, the third largest Church in Brazil, Fortress of Nossa Senhora da Assuncao; a seventeenth century fort, Centro Dragão do Mar de Arte e Cultura (Sea Dragon Art and Culture Centre) and Beach Park; Brazil's largest water park.

Belo Horizonte

Belo Horizonte is positioned on the Southeast region of the country, and is the capital of Brazil's state of Minas Gerais. With a population of over 2.4 million people, Belo Horizonte is the most populous city in Minas Gerais State and is equally, the 6th most populous city in Brazil.

It is one of the few Brazilian Cities which was duly planned before being constructed around 1890's. It is an epitome of enviable scenes and striking architecture such as the Pampulha complex and the Liberty Square. It has most of its streets and avenues lined up with trees.

The Population Crisis Committee of the United Nations had recognized Belo Horizonte as one of Latin America's Metropolises with the best quality of life. Surrounded by the *Serra do Curral* Mountain range, Belo Horizonte is titled "Garden City" for being one of the most arboreal cities in Brazil.

According to the International Congress and Conference Association's (ICCA) rankings, Belo Horizonte is among the top Brazilian cities that most receives international events. It is equally a reference city in business and health tourism matters.

Cuiabá

With a population of over 600,000 inhabitants, Cuiabá is the capital of Mato Grosso State.

Cuiabá is popularly known as 'the Green City'; a rare name it has earned because it is the region where Brazil's three most important characteristic ecosystems meet: the Cerrado, the Pantanal wetlands, and the Amazon.

Manaus

Manaus is the capital of the Amazonas State, and is a gateway to the biggest tropical habitat on earth: the Amazon Rainforest. This makes Manaus a popular destination for ecotourism.

It is equally, in Manaus where the dark waters of Rio Negro (Black River) and muddy waters of Rio Solimões converge to form a stunning and an unforgettable scene.

Other valuable features found in Manaus is the Opera House, *Teatro Amazonas* (Amazon theater), and the old striking Rio Negro Palace. Manaus has steadily grown over the years and is today one of Brazil's largest cities. The city has a population of over 1.9 million inhabitants.

Curitiba

Curitiba is a capital of The State of Paraná. Curitiba emerged as Brazil's perfect example of what cities can become as due to good management that results to responsible development and economic growth.

'Curitiba is wealthy and beautiful'. It is one of the favorite cities to live in by most well-off members of the Brazilian community. Some of the beautiful attractions in Curitiba include: The Oscar Niemeyer Museum, Tanguá and Barigüi parks, Ópera de Arame and most significantly, its Botanical gardens houses some of the world's rare plant species.

Aracaju

Found in the northeastern part of the country, Aracaju is the capital of the State of Sergipe.

It is modestly populated and is known throughout Brazil for: its modern outlook and it's well planned and coordinated carnival celebrations and many other festivals it hosts.

Porto Alegre

Porto Alegre is famous for its spectacular beaches and lots of striking sceneries. It immensely contributes towards the Brazilian economy, culture and politics.

With a growing population of over 1.5 inhabitants, Porto Alegre is the capital of the State of Rio Grande do Sul.

The city is beautifully positioned on the banks of Lago Guaíba, at a point where five rivers converge to create the vast *Lagoa dos Patos*.

Porto Alegre enjoys subtropical climate with a mixture of varied cultures. Thousands of immigrants from Portugal, Poland, Germany, and Italy have found home in Porto Allegre.

Recife

Recife is located in the Northeastern region of Brazil, and is the capital and largest city of the state of Pernambuco. The city received its name from the coral reefs that line its beautiful coasts Recife was anciently, built as a port city, and is currently, a famous a hub for exportation of Sugar, Coffee and Cotton. By the year 2013, Recife had more than 1.6million inhabitants.

Recife has some of the best infrastructures in Brazil, and an unforgettable spectacular scenery, culture and beaches. Recife's beach of Porto de Galinhas has continually won several awards as the best beach in Brazil.

"The Recife area has only recently become a tourist attraction, and has come to be popularly known as the Venice of Brazil for its many connecting bridges, canals, and small windy streets."…
{www.braziltravelinformation.com}.

Natal

Natal is popularly referred to as 'The City of Sun' (*Cidade do Sol),* and also 'The City of The Dune'. Natal is the capital of State of Rio Grande do Norte.

It has a warm climate with average daily temperatures of 28°C.
Natal is the closest South American city to Europe, a feat that puts it in an advantageous position in receiving more international tourists.

Florianópolis

Voted by The New York Times as 'The Party Destination of The Year 2009', Florianópolis has since then become synonymous with the title of 'The Best Place To Live In Brazil'.

That publicity opened up Florianópolis as a destination point to most tourists from Europe, South America and even North America.

Florianópolis is the capital of an island State of Santa Catarina and is cherished for being a city which offers high quality of life. The city is a popular destination for island excursions that have a more secluded and serene backgrounds.

Boa Vista

Boa Vista is the capital of Brazilian State of Roraima. It is the only capital found on the north of equator. The city stands out as it was carefully designed and erected with a radial plan.

João Pessoa

João Pessoa is the capital of Paraíba, a State in the northeast region of Brazil. Founded in the year 1585, the city is popularly referred to as 'the city where the sun rises first.' It is equally home to some of the great Brazilian writers and poets such as Augusto dos Anjos.

Belém

Belém, literally referred to as Bethlehem, is the capital of the state of Pará. Belém is the Brazilian doorway to the Amazon River.

Campo Grande

Campo Grande popularly referred to as *Cidade Morena*. ("Swarthy City"), is the capital of the Brazilian State of Mato Grosso do Sul. The city is found in the centralwest region of Brazil, and has obtained its nickname out of the reddish-brown color of the region's soil.

Municipalities

Due to the country's geographical vastness and huge population, Brazil has an allocation of more than five thousand, six hundred (5,600) Municipalities.

Each Municipality acts as an administrative division of the State in which it is located.

Each State has an average of more than two hundred (200) Municipalities. Roraima State however, has less than twenty (20), Municipalities while Minas Gerais State has over eight hundred (800) Municipalities.

Note: According to the provisions of the country's Law, the Federal District, in which Brasília falls, cannot be divided into Municipal areas.

Each Municipality acts as a Local Government. They are headed by Mayors and have legislative bodies charged with responsibilities of handling legal aspects of running their respective Municipal Jurisdictions. But notably, Courts are organized at State's levels. These Local Governments are autonomous in their operations, hence securely shielded from any external political influence.

Municipalities collect taxes from their residents, and are also entitled to receipt of funds from their respective States.

Some of The Famous Brazilians

Over the years, Brazil has produced a number of world's well-known and respected personalities in diverse fields: Sports, Arts, Politics, Literature, Science, Religion, Science etc.

Below are a few of Brazil's well-known and respected personalities.

Oscar Ribeiro de Almeida Niemeyer

Oscar Ribeiro de Almeida Niemeyer was popularly referred to as the father of Brazilian architecture and arts. Literally, *'He is the man who built Brasilia'.*

Born on the 15TH December, 1907, Niemeyer earned both local and international accolades for some of his distinctive and incredible building designs. Interestingly, Niemeyer is equally famous for achieving a feat of being married at the age of 99 years to second wife, Vera Lucia Cabriera; his assistant, in the year 2006 after the death of his first wife in the year 2004.

Some of Oscar's notable designs include: Rio's Sambadrome, Museum of The Republic in Brasilia, The United Nation's Headquarters in New York, The Tombstone for Carlos Marighella in Salvador da Bahia, the Serpentine Gallery Summer Pavilion in Kensington Gardens in London, and the Niteroi Contemporary Art Museum in Rio de Jenairo.

Oscar Ribeiro de Almeida Niemeyer died on the 5TH of December 2012, aged 104 years.

Edson Arantes do Nascimento – Pelé

Brazilian football has come a long way. Undeniably, Brazil is home to some of the world's best footballers. If tabled, the list of current successful Brazilian footballers and football legends can be very long!

Notably, born on 21ST October 1940, Edson Arantes do Nascimento – Popularly referred to as Pelé, is one of the famous Brazilian football heroes. He was named after the famous American inventor, Thomas Edison. Later, his parents decided to remove letter 'i' from his name and called him Edson. However, that change could not be effectively effected since it failed to be corrected on his birth certificate, and hence, many of his other vital certificates retained the original name of Edison instead of Edson.

Pelé, worked hard on the pitch and the payout was to win the prestigious World Cup trophy for Brazil, three times (1958, 1962 and 1970), making him the only Brazilian player to achieve such an enviable feat. He was the all-time leading goal scorer for Brazil.

During his football career, he was honored by being voted as the Football Player of the Century by the International Federation of Football History and Statistics (IFFHS) in 1999. In the same year, he was elected by IOC as an 'athlete of the century' and later named by the Time Magazine as one amongst the 100 most influential people in the 20th Century. He was more often referred to as 'The Black Pearl' (Perola Negra), 'The King of Football' (O Rei do Futebol), 'The King Pele' (O Rei Pelé).

Rubens Gonclaves Barrichello

Born on the 23rd of May, 1972, in São Paulo, Brazil, Rubens Barrichello is one of Brazil's motorsports icons and the most experienced Formula One Driver.

He shares his birthday with his father who is also named Rubens. However, Rubens Barrichello was also known as Rubinho (a Portuguese word for little Rubens).

At the 2008 Turkish Grand Prix, Barrichelo achieved a feat of being the world's most experienced driver. And in the year 2010, Barrichello became the event's first driver to achieve grand prix of 300 starts.

He retired from racing in Formula One at the end of the year 2011 after having started 322 races in his fulfilling racing career.

Miguel Nicolelis

Born on March 7th 1961 in São Paulo, Miguel Angelo Laporta Nicolelis, MD, PHD, is best known for his pioneering work in "reading monkey thought". He is one of the world's most respected neuroscientists.

He was instrumental in founding the International Institute for Neuroscience of Natal.

In the year 2011, he was appointed by Pope Benedict XVI as an ordinary member of the Pontifical Academy of Science.

Carmen Miranda

The late Maria do Carmo Miranda da Cunha, GCIH – (The Order of Prince Henry the Navigator) was born on the 9th of February the year 1909.

She was famed as a samba dancer, Samba singer and as an actress. Carmen Miranda acted on Broadway and in the Hollywood.

When she died out of heart attack in California's Beverly Hills in the year 1955, over 65,000 Brazilians attended her burial ceremony which took place in Rio de Janeiro.

Fernando Meirelles

Fernando Ferreira Meirelles was born on the 9th of November,1955, in São Paulo.

A Film Director, Producer and Screenwriter, Fernando is one of the few Brazilians in the film industry who have worn several world accolades.

- As a film director in the movie 'City of Gold', Fernando was nominated for an academy award in the category of Best Director, in the year 2004.
- The 'Constant Gardener' also enabled him to be nominated for a Golden Globe award in same category of Best Director, in the year 2005.

Francisco Costa

The enviable design company 'Calvin Klain', usually abbreviated as CK, has stood out over the years, due to immense contributions of Francisco Costa as the company's Women's Creative Director.

Born on the 10th of May, 1964, Francisco Costa has won several world accolades:

- *He won a Women's Wear Designer of the Year awards in the years 2006, and 2008, in Council of Fashion Designers of America.*
- *And in the year 2009, he won Cooper-Hewitt National Fashion Design Award.*

Princess Isabel

Born on 29Th July 1846, in Rio de Janeiro, Princess Isabel was the eldest daughter of Emperor Dom Pedro II and Empress Dona Teresa Cristina.

Princess Isabel died on 14th November 1921 is famous for her golden signature on *Lei Áurea* or the Golden Law; which marked the end of slavery in Brazil.

Holidays Observed In Brazil

Below are the most common holidays observed by Cariocas:

1st January: New Year's Day (New Year Celebrations).

February/March: Carnival Celebrations (This varies every year but must be staged before *Lent*).

March/April: Easter.

13th April: Day of The Brazilian Flag.

21st April: Remembrance of Tiradentes.

1st May: International Workers Day (Labour Day).

May/June: Corpus Christi.

7th September: Brazil's Independence Day.

12th October: Nossa Senhora Aparecida.

2nd November: All Souls Day (The Day of the Dead).

5th November: Proclamation of the Republic.

25th December: Christmas Day (Christmas Celebrations).

Sports

As a result of its temperate conditions throughout the year, Brazil has a perfect weather condition to support many sporting activities.

The varied sporting activities found in Brazil include:

Football

Football or Soccer is undoubtedly, Brazil's undisputed number one sporting activity. It is said that the first thing any Brazilian child would do immediately, after learning to walk is to play soccer.

The Brazil's National Football Team is also known as Seleção. However, they are popularly referred to as the Samba Boys.

Brazil is an enviable home to world's football greats: Pele, Garrincha, Didi, Vava, Zagallo, Tostão, Zico, Jairzinho, Carlos Alberto, Socrates, Bebeto, Kaka, Neymar Romario, Cafu, Ronaldinho, Ronaldo, Roberto Carlos. ....and the list is endless. Due to their unique skills and techniques in handling balls in the football field, some of these Brazilian players have earned the title of 'football magicians'.

Edson Arantes do Nascimento, popularly referred to as Pelé, is the record youngest goal-scorer in FIFA World Cup history and the only player to have won three FIFA World Cups in the Brazilian history.

Brazil's Ronaldo, is the top goal-scorer in FIFA World Cup history with a record 15 goals. (Prior to 2014 FIFA World Cup). Brazil's football team has won the coveted world cup trophy a record number of 5 times; in the years, 1958, 1962, 1970, 1994, and 2002. And over the years, Brazil hasn't failed to feature in any world cup football event. This demonstrates how deeply-rooted, football has its foundations within the walls of this South American jewel.

Brazil's Marta is the most decorated female football player in the world, having won Five Women's World Player of the Year awards and equally, being a joint top goal-scorer in FIFA Women's World Cup history with 14 goals.

Volleyball

Volleyball is the second most popular sports in Brazil after football. The Brazilian National volleyball teams (both men and women), have over the years, continuously, featured in the Volleyball World Cup, Volleyball World Championships, and as well as in the Olympics.

Basketball

Basketball is the third most popular sports in Brazil after Football and Volleyball.

Brazil's National Basketball Team is respected in the international basketball arenas and has continued to produce players who are equally respected at international levels.

Oscar Schmidt is one of Brazil's greatest men basketball players, while Hortencia Marcari represents the greatest women basketball players in the same country.

In the years 1959 and 1963, Brazil's Men Basketball National Team won the World Basketball Championship. The team has equally won a record number of medals in the Olympics, Pan-American Games, and in the American Championship.

Motorsports

In motorsports, Brazil is the home to the world's bests: The great Rubens Barrichello, Felipe Masa, Bruno Senna, Ayrton Senna and many more.

Brazil has continued to be an indispensable competitor in Formula One, Stock Car Brasil Fórmula Truck, and in the South American Formula Three. Brazilians also participate in motorbike racing e.g. the MotoGP.

Tennis

Brazil usually sends out Tennis Players to important world tennis events such as US Open and Wimbledon. Over the years, the country has continued to witness some of the world's tennis players emerge out of its boundaries.

Rugby

Brazilians love rugby, but their rugby national team is yet to achieve meaningful accomplishments; if any comparison would be drawn with the country's success in football.

Foot Volley

Foot Volley is derived from two sporting activities: Football and Volleyball. It is a game played mostly, in beaches under volleyball net, or even in the absence of the net.

The only unique rule to this game is that the participants can only use their feet to pass a ball from one side of the net/play to the other side. Use of hands is prohibited and may be penalized (if it's a competition) by awarding points to the opposite competing side.

Beach Football

This type of football is common within the numerous Brazilian beaches.

It has the same rules as the ones applicable to real football game, only that the sizes of the field and the goal posts aren't standard. And participants are usually bare-footed with beach sands as the field setting.

Beach Volleyball

This type of volleyball is equally prevalent within the beaches. Its participants usually wear beach-fitting attires (bikinis and shorts), and mostly, play barefooted.

Martial Arts

Capoeira is a popular form of martial arts in Brazil. It is a beautifully choreographed, acrobatic and more often accompanied by music.

Other sports in Brazil include: Handball, Boxing, Water Polo, Horse Riding, Hockey, Golf, Judo, American Football, Skate Boarding, Athletics, Sailing, Cricket, Surfing, Chess, Badminton …. and much more.

Dances

The Brazilian dance has greatly been influenced by centuries of entrenched local diverse cultures.

Brazilians use dance as a means to; freely express their inward feelings, to tell both old and new tales, and to pass across messages in more personal ways.

Over the years, Brazilians have continued to perfect and have even formalized certain dance styles. Such dance styles have today grown to be popular amongst the Brazilians, and have even grown beyond the borders of the country.

The famous Brazilian Dances include:

The Samba

This is the most popular and famous dance in Brazil. Even visiting tourists in Brazil always thirst to be treated to a Samba-dance experience. It is regarded as the hallmark and a representation of Brazil's hidden treasure and beauty.

The history of Samba's origin is closely associated with the ancient slaves who were brought into the country between 16th and 19th centuries. It is believed that Samba originated from the beats and custom of those ancient slaves. However, the upper class Brazilians, (in terms of social status), often viewed this type of dance as indecent, thereby forcing the slaves to perform it in the undergrounds and in other private places. However, it was during the 1920's that Samba eventually gained its popularity and subsequent wide acceptance.

The Lundu

One of the famous old-aged and preserved dance styles in Brazil. It is believed to have been the most popular dance in the 17th century. For perfect exhibition, this dance is usually accompanied by a piano, drums, guitar and more often include castanets.

The Capoeira

This dance style is believed to have a link to martial arts, and an accompaniment of music is very essential in its performance. It has a number of kicks and movements that are similar to those in martial arts. It has to be carefully practiced and arranged in order to exhibit skill and discipline during its performance.

The Carimbo and Lambada

It is worthy to note that the Lambada is born out of Carimbo. The Carimbo is regarded as a traditional folk dance, which is a blend of African, Portuguese and other western and European cultures. Many people today refer to it as a true exhibition of the real Brazilian Culture. The Carimbo dance is popularly, known for its bodily and sexual nature.

The Forro.

This is the most popular dance in the North Eastern region of Brazil. It has a well synchronized set of movements that require a partner in order to make it livelier. It has many styles and is usually conducted to a music which includes the use of accordion and the triangle.

Time, Electricity, And Measurements

Time

Brazil majorly experiences three natural time zones. Brasilia, Sao Paulo, Salvador Rio de Janeiro and most parts of Brazil's inland are usually two hours ahead of EST, or -3GMT.

The Amazonas, Mato Grosso do Sul and Mato Grosso are one hour a head of EST.

The western parts of the Amazon follow EST.

Electricity

Just like most South American countries, electricity in Brazil ranges from 100volts to 240 volts. However, due to frequent power surges which occur in some of the Cities, it is usually advisable to have a power adaptor or a power surge enabled power sockets to counter those power surges

Measurements

As a standard for measurements, Brazil adopted the use of metric system way back in the colonial era. Weights are measured in kilograms (1kg = 2.2 pounds, 1 pound = 0.45 kilograms, I ton = 2204 pounds). Other measurements are: I mile equaling 1.15 kilometers, I square mile = 2.6 square kilometers and I acre = 0.4 hectares. To convert degree F to degrees C = (F-32)/1.8 etc.

Currency/Money, Taxes, And Tipping

Currency /Money

The Brazilian currency is known as Real.

In Brazil, there is well spread and easy accessibility of services of financial institutions. ATMs are widely distributed within the City. It is safe and convenient to use credit cards, however, buying goods in local currency will most definitely give you value for your money.

Master cards and Visas are equally widely accepted by most institutions and merchants in Brazil i.e. hotels, clubs, lodges, restaurants, supermarkets etc.

Taxes

Most goods available for purchase within Brazil usually have tax inclusive prices.

Tipping

Hotel/Bar/Restaurant Bills: You are expected to pay a service charge of about 10% on your hotel, restaurant, or bar bills. You are free to give any additional tip as a way of showing your appreciation for the service enjoyed.

Taxis: It is not compulsory to give taxi drivers any tip. You can do so on your own will, and as a way of showing your appreciation for the service offered.

Bellhops: Bellhops usually get tipped at an average of $ 0.60 per bag.

Attractions In Brazil

Brazil offers a warm discovery, and vast array of unforgettable tourist attraction sites. The country is endowed uniquely, with unlimited beauty, sceneries, sights, tastes, and sounds.

The major tourist attractions in Brazil are divided into two:

- *Natural Attractions.*
- *Artificial (man-made) Attractions.*

Natural Attractions

- Superb, awesome, beautiful and stunning, would be the least adjectives to use in defining the thousands of miles of Brazil's beaches. The beaches colorfully lie on Brazil's vast coastline, where emerald blue waters fuse with the golden and white sandy beaches.
- The Amazon River
- The Pantanal.
- The Amazon Jungle
- The Rain Forests
- Millions of plant and animal species
- Waterfalls; especially the world's largest waterfall, the Iguaçu falls.

Artificial Attractions

- The state of art buildings and architectures found in Brasília. Notably, Brasília has been accorded a World Heritage Site Status by UNESCO. An accomplishment that is the envy of many other cities round the world.
- Salvador de Bahia – a city with striking Buildings, Culture, Music, Food, Beaches.
- Itaipu Dam on Brazil's border with Paraguay.
- Christ the Redeemer Statue in Rio de Janeiro.

- Sambadrome in Rio de Janeiro and in other cities in Brazil.

The above list of natural and artificial attractions are just about tip into Brazil's unlimited attractions. Some of the country's most common attractions are covered in the coming pages.

World Heritage Sites In Brazil

Because of their historical importance, cultural and conservation related significances, the following sites/ places in Brazil have been accorded the status of World Heritage Sites by the responsible body; UNESCO.

- Historic Town of Ouro Preto.
- Historic Centre of the Town of Olinda.
- Jesuit Missions of the Guaranis: San Ignacio Mini, Santa Ana, Nuestra Señora de Loreto and Santa Maria Mayor (Argentina), Ruins of Sao Miguel das Missoes (Brazil).
- Historic Centre of Salvador de Bahia.
- Sanctuary of Bom Jesus do Congonhas.
- Iguaçu National Park.
- Brasilia.
- Serra da Capivara National Park.
- Historic Centre of São Luís.
- Atlantic Forest South-East Reserves.
- Discovery Coast Atlantic Forest Reserves.
- Historic Centre of the Town of Diamantina.
- Central Amazon Conservation Complex.
- Pantanal Conservation Area.
- Brazilian Atlantic Islands: Fernando de Noronha and Atol das Rocas Reserves.

- Cerrado Protected Areas: Chapada dos Veadeiros and Emas National Parks.
- Historic Centre of the Town of Goiás.
- São Francisco Square in the Town of São Cristóvào.
- Rio de Janeiro: Carioca Landscapes between the Mountain and the Sea.

(UNESCO:- Brazil's World Heritage Sites)

Brazil's Major Tourist Attraction Sites

Christ the Redeemer Statue.

The famous Christ the Redeemer statue is situated in Rio de Janeiro.

Christ the Redeemer Statue is considered the largest Art Deco statue in the world. Its planning and subsequent construction is believed to have begun in the early 1920's, the momentous period of Art Deco movement. In 2014, the statue completed its 83rd anniversary, having being officially inaugurated in 1931.

Christ the Redeemer Statue is in records as one of the modern Seven Wonders of the World. The statue; an image of Jesus Christ with both arms outstretched, and watching calmly over Rio de Janeiro, is beautifully perched on the peak of Corcovado Mountain, whose height is over 700 meters.

The Statue's height is over 35 meters, excluding over 8 meters of its pedestal. The stretched arms of the statue are estimated to be over 28 meters.

Since its erection, Christ the Redeemer Statue has over the years immensely stood out as an enviable landmark in both the City of Rio de Janeiro and in Brazil as Country. Its contribution to the

Brazilian economy as a major tourist attraction site has undoubtedly, been immense.

Visitors to the Statue can opt to either climb up hundreds of steps, or use a tram ride or an elevator.

Iguazu Falls/Iguassu Falls/Iguaçu Falls

The Iguazu Falls is another Brazilian marvel. Located on the Brazilian border with Argentina, and on Iguazu River, the waterfall can be directly accessed through the towns of Puerto Iguazu and Foz do Iguassu in both Argentina and Brazil respectively.

Over the years, this world's wonder has continued to attract many tourists to Brazil and will continue to do so for many years to come.

The waterfall is just a two hour flight away from Brazil's city of Sao Paulo.

Physically, the waterfalls appear to be within the Argentinean boundary, but its panoramic view is best from the Brazilian boundary. Iguacu Falls when viewed from the Brazilian side fully displays a full and naked beauty of this world's wonder.

Iguazu falls is uniquely surrounded by the Argentinean Iguazú National Park and Brazil's Iguaçu National Park; which are both recognized World Heritage Sites by UNESCO.

In order to experience an un-forgettable tour of Iguacu falls, tourists are often challenged to witness the first-hand-marvels of the fall's *Garganta del Diablo* (The Devil's Throat); the greatest site and the most breathtaking view of the waterfalls.

The Amazon

The Amazon is found in the State of Amazonas and is home to diverse flora and fauna. The world's second longest river, and world's largest river by volume, the Amazon River, has given room to the existence of the wild Amazon Jungle together with its wild inhabitants.

Some of the highlights of the Amazon region include:

- A stunning spot for watching the convergence of the black waters of river Rio Negro mixing with muddy waters of river Rio Salimoes, near the city of Manaus. Manaus has the biggest airport in the region, hence, serves as a base for most trips into the Amazon jungle.

- The breathtaking firsthand experience of the Amazon jungle with its wildlife. The Amazon basin is believed to be home to more than half of the remaining earth's rain forests.

- Firsthand experience of the unique lifestyle of the local inhabitants of the Amazon forests.

Some engaging activities within the Amazon include; *hunting, fishing and deep jungle exploration*. The Amazon houses thousands of fish species, with new ones being discovered year in year out.

Within the Amazon, there are many Eco-Lodges which would conveniently hand any visiting party an opportunity to experience the 'real wild side' of the Amazon. There are also Cruise Ships and multiple circuits around the jungle awaiting persons interested in real adventure.

The Carnival Celebrations

Carnivals in Brazil are an unforgettable experience of the real beauty, culture and sounds of this unique South American country.

Brazilians believe that the origins of Carnival Celebrations stretch way back into the periods of beginnings of humanity. The carnivals are annually celebrated before Lent; a Catholic Holiday. Before the actual start of Carnival celebrations, there are usually some days set aside for rehearsals and city parades.

Carnival celebration in Brazil is regarded as the world's largest celebration of its kind. It is a dazzling period of steamy fun and partying in every corner of Brazil.
Witnessing or taking part in any Brazilian Carnival is an unforgettable and a non-regrettable life experience. Big Carnival celebrations are usually witnessed in the Cities of Rio de Janeiro, Salvador de Bahia, Olinda and Recife. In these cities together with others, there are specially built venues known as Sambadromes, where the climax of the Carnival celebration are usually organized.

Fernando de Noronha

This is Brazil's hidden jewel. Located on the northeastern coast of Brazil, Fernando de Noronha is a beautiful archipelago with vast, secluded and undiscovered: wildlife, serene beaches and stunning landscapes.

The area is least populated and is a haven for divers due to its clear and warm waters.

Ipanema Beach

Ipanema beach gained its fame out of *'The Girl From Ipanema'* song by Antonio Carlos Jobim.

Brazil has many beaches; however, Ipanema beach is one of the tourists' favorite. It is well supplied with enough hotels, restaurants, cafés and lodgings. Equally, it is strategically surrounded with well stocked shopping malls, full of divergent souvenirs.

Ipanema beach is the place to be for watching Rio's stunning views of sunrises and sunsets by the beach. Without any doubt, Ipanema beach is one of the best urban beaches in the world. It is filled with clean and clear waters; making it a paradise for swimming. Along the beach, you can never miss to spot tourists and locals engaged in beach football, beach foot volleyball, beach volleyball, and sunbathing.

To access Ipanema beach, the nearest Airport; Santos Dumont Domestic Airport, is roughly 15-20 minutes drive away. Still, you can use the Tom Jobim International Airport, which is approximately 40 minutes drive away. The beauty of these two airports is that they are constantly fed with taxis and buses which conveniently, shuttle people to and from the beach.

The Pantanal

Lying in the central-western region of Brazil, the Pantanal is the world's largest wetland.

The Pantanal offers an unforgettable bird-watching experience, and is home to one of the largest wild animals' population in South America.

Did you know that one can tour the Amazon rainforest without a guarantee of seeing any wild animal? However, in the Pantanal, seeing wildlife is guaranteed. The hawks, Caimans, Otters, Jaguars, Tapirs, monkeys, herons, and anacondas are in their thousands within the Pantanal.

A trip through the Pantanal is usually taken through use of boats, four-wheel drive vehicles, horses and even by walking.

A nearby Chupada dos Guimaraes offers an amazing hiking trails with cool views along. Most visitors to the Pantanal usually access it from Cuiaba, which is located in the southern part of the Pantanal.

Some Brazilian Cities worth visiting

Brazil's cities are a beehive of rich cultures, vast biodiversity and stunning landscapes. Notably, all cities in Brazil are worthy destinations for any tourist, however, there are certain cities within this South American country, which are worthy of being given special attention, due to their immense contribution towards enabling Brazil to feature in the international arena as a tourist's favorite..

Some of the Cities which top this list have already been highlighted (*Refer to the topic on Cities*). The already highlighted Brazilian cities worthy of visit are:

- **Rio de Janeiro.**
- **Florianópolis**
- **Salvador.**
- **Cuiabá**
- **Manaus.**
- **Brasília.**
- **Fortaleza.**

- Porto Alegre.
- São Paulo.
- Curitiba.
- Belo Horizonte.
- Natal.

Since Brazil is geographical vast and has been partitioned into regions, it is usually advisable to check the cities located within the regions of Brazil where you intend to visit.

Other Brazilian Cities/Towns Worth Visiting

Petrópolis

Strategically located at the foothills of Serra dos Órgãos National Park, Petrópolis is a renowned winter resort town. It is famously referred to as 'The Imperial City of Brazil'. In the 19th century, Petrópolis was the preferred home of both the Brazilian Emperors and the wealthy, during summer.

Petrópolis means 'City of Peter'. It was named in honor of Emperor Pedro II, the country's second monarch, and son of Pedro I. Significantly, between 1894 and 1902, Petrópolis served as the official capital of state of Rio de Janeiro.

It is roughly forty to fifty minutes drive from Rio de Janeiro City. And unlike the densely populated City center, Petrópolis is less populated, with serene surrounding.

One of its famous attractions is the former Summer Palace of the second Brazilian Emperor (now converted into the famous Imperial Museum of Brazil. The Palácio Quitandinha (a historic former luxury resort hotel), The Cathedral of Petrópolis, and the Crystal Glasshouse are other worthy places to visit in Petrópolis.

Paraty/Parati

Parati or Paraty is found along the coast of the State of Rio de Janeiro. It is a favorite spot for tourists within the State of Rio de Janeiro. It is endowed with lush tropical forests, emerald blue sea waters, remarkable mountains and waterfalls. Just like Petrópolis, Parati is also a former colony of the Portuguese.

Olinda

Located in the Atlantic coast in the northeastern region, Olinda is a historic city within the Brazilian state of Pernambuco. The Historic Centre of the Town of Olinda (its downtown area) is in UNESCO's records as a World Heritage Site.

Olinda is one of Brazil's best preserved colonial cities with a number of churches. Carnivals in Olinda are celebrated in almost similar manner as the Portuguese Carnivals, but with a spice of African influenced dance styles.

Ouro Petro

Ouro Petro *'black gold'* is located in the State of Minas Gerais. Over the years, Ouro Petro still stands today as one of the best preserved colonial towns with the colonial architecture being the benchmark for erecting modern buildings. Interestingly, Ouro Petro still has some of its churches decorated with gold.

Ouro Petro is an epitome of preserved colonial architecture with rich culture and divergent religious background.

Travel Requirements

Passport And Visa

To gain entry into any part of Brazil, visitors are required to have valid passports and visas. Passports are obtained from various countries' immigration offices or departments, or designated offices entrusted with responsibilities of issuing such documents.

Brazilian Visas are granted by Brazilian Embassies, or Brazilian Consulates located in most countries all over the world. The Visas are normally approved for duration of three months (90 days). Once issued, you can only use it to gain entry into Brazil within the 90 days from the stipulated date, and not after the expiry of the 90 days. You can't use an expired Visa to gain entry into Brazil.

Once you've entered Brazil, you can request for an extension of your Visa for another 90 days; bringing the total duration of time you can spend in Brazil to 180 days (6 months). However, you must make the request at least two weeks before the expiry of your Visa.

In case you wish to travel to Brazil: as a tourist, to attend a conference, to attend a business meeting or seminar, to attend an arts or music event, or to attend a sports-related event, you must first be issued with a Visa.

Visa Exemptions (Tourist Visas)

Over the years, a good number of visitors to Brazil have been coming from Argentina, Italy and United States of America.

In bid to attract more visitors, the country has taken bold steps to waive Tourist Visa requirements for many countries including: *Andorra, Argentina, Austria, Bahamas, Barbados, Belgium, Bolivia, Bulgaria, Chile, Colombia, Costa Rica, Croatia, Czech Republic, Denmark, Ecuador, Finland, France, Germany, Greece, Guatemala,*

Guyana, Honduras, Hungary, Iceland, Ireland, Israel, Italy, Liechtenstein, Luxembourg, Macau, Malaysia, Monaco, Morocco, Namibia, the Netherlands, New Zealand, Norway, Panama, Paraguay, Peru, the Philippines, Poland, Portugal, Romania, San Marino, Slovakia, Slovenia, South Africa, South Korea, the Sovereign Order of Malta (citizens of Malta must have a visa), Spain, Suriname, Sweden, Switzerland, Thailand, Trinidad & Tobago, Tunisia, Turkey, United Kingdom, Uruguay, the Vatican and Venezuela.

Nonetheless, visitors from some of these countries and many others may still be required to have a business visa even though they may be exempt from tourist visas. The most recent and updated information on countries whose citizens enjoy the Tourist Visa exemption, together with other visa related information can be accessed from various embassies and consulates of Brazil. Notably, many of these embassies and consulates have updated such information on their websites; for ease of access by the public.

Requirements For Visa Application

In order to apply for a Brazilian Visa, you need the below:

- A valid passport of not less than 6 months from the date of its first issue. The passport <u>Must</u> not be damaged, defaced, or even soiled.
- Duly filled and correctly signed Visa application form.
- A passport size photograph (carry two just in case).
- International certificate of vaccination (where necessary).
- In case you are taking part in a conference, a seminar, a sports event, an art or music event, etc, you must show proof of letter of invitation from the organizers of such event(s).
- Receipt of payment of application/processing fee
- Copies (and show the originals) of the onward and return air tickets, and or proof of means of support during your

stay in the country. Notably, Pay slips from your current employer, or bank account statements or credit card statements are usually accepted as proof.

Entry For Children or Minors

Persons under the age of 18 are classified as minors. In case they wish to travel to any part of Brazil; unaccompanied, or with one parent or guardian, or with a third-party, a written consent or authorization, in Portuguese language, and authenticated by relevant Brazilian Embassy or Consulate must be obtained from the non-traveling parent or guardian.

The authorization must clearly indicate that the non-traveling parent or guardian has granted the minor permission to travel with the accompanying party.

For children between 3 months to 6 years, proof of vaccination against polio is compulsory. (A vaccination letter/card/booklet/document form a local recognized hospital/clinic/health facility may effectively serve as proof).

Dual Citizenship

Citizens from other countries who hold Brazilian Nationality must obtain Brazilian passports from relevant Brazilian Embassies or Consulates. They are never issued with Tourist Visas as they are regarded as Brazilians, and subject to the Brazilian laws.

Vaccinations/Immunizations

If you wish to travel to the areas around the jungle, vaccinations or preventative measures against Malarial attack is advisable.

You must provide an International Certificate of Vaccination against yellow fever if within three months prior to traveling to Brazil, you have visited, or have been in transit through any of the these countries: *Angola, Benin, Bolivia, Burkina Faso, Burundi, Cameroon, Central African Republic, Chad, Colombia, Cote d'Ivoire, Democratic Republic of the Congo, Ecuador, Equatorial Guinea, Ethiopia, French Guiana, Gabon, Gambia, Ghana, Guinea, Guinea Bissau, Guyana, Kenya, Liberia, Mali, Mauritania, Niger, Nigeria, Panama, Peru, Republic of the Congo (Brazzaville), Rwanda, Sao Tome and Principe, Senegal, Sierra Leone, Somalia, Sudan, Suriname, Tanzania, Togo, Trinidad and Tobago, Uganda, Venezuela.*

If you would wish to travel to a number of Brazilian cities, it's best recommended you get vaccinated against yellow fever.

Taking Pets To Brazil

In case you wish to take pets (Dogs and Cats), to Brazil, you must ensure that:

- The pets are duly vaccinated against rabies (you should have a relevant certificate of vaccination against rabies).
- They must also be in possession of a Public Health Certificate from the respective country where the pet is originating from.

What You Must Do When You Enter/Leave Brazil

Once your Visa is approved, you will be provided with an Embarkation and Disembarkation card which you must correctly fill and append your signature to. Upon your arrival, or when leaving, Brazil, submit theses documents to relevant Brazilian authorities.

What To Do In Case You Are Lost

When preparing to make a solo trip to Brazil, always have within your pack, a map, or some sort of local guide which will enable you to have easy reference towards your destination(s).

However, in case you get lost along the way, do not panic, or physically show that you are lost. Just stay calm and boldly, walk to any nearby restaurant, hotel, or any open government facility, and ask for help.

The beauty of living is in getting lost, and reaching out to others for help. Even when seeking for the guidance of others towards your destination, always stay alert and trust your sixth sense.

Too, always have in your possession the emergency contact numbers of the local Police, or of the local Administrators of the nearby places you intend to visit. Having such numbers in your possession may prove handy in such scaring moments.

The Smoking Rule, And Taxis

The smoking rule

The legal age for sale or consumption of tobacco in Brazil is 18 years.

Brazil has adopted the smoke-free law for all workplaces and public areas. Flavored cigarettes, including menthol cigarettes are outlawed. Smoking is therefore, prohibited in all indoor and enclosed public spaces. Such Places include shopping malls, movie theaters, schools and government places, health facilities etc.

Brazil has specifically designated certain areas to act as Smoking Zones. Notably, relevant fines are applied to persons who do not abide by the smoke law. However, some states have even banned the use of such designated smoking zones.

Taxis

Taxis can easily be accessed in all Brazilian cities, municipalities, and towns. Preferably, you should use the licensed or registered taxis. Notably, several taxis are fitted with taximeters which usefully convert the amount of time taken and distance traveled into fare charge.

Most taxi drivers can comfortably communicate in English. However, should you come across a taxi driver unable to communicate in English, or in any of your preferred language, it is advisable to write down the address of your intended destination and show it to the driver.

As an appreciation for the service offered, you can tip the taxi driver. However, tipping any taxi driver is not mandatory.

Some of The Most Notorious Cheats/Scams In Brazil

Today, no country can authoritatively, claim to be a public scams-free arena. Therefore, Brazil, just like any other country, has some forms of cheats/scams which are well orchestrated and prevalent within most of its urban suburbs.

Below are some forms of such notorious cheats/scams:

The famous biblical 'good Samaritan'

This is the most common cheat reported by most tourists and even locals. When an individual looks lost, and might be having difficulty in communication, a bystander may approach with seemingly, 'innocent intentions' to help out. However, in many cases, such innocent offers of unsolicited help have turned ugly as the 'good Samaritan' convincingly lures his or her innocent victim into robbers' trap.

Whenever you realize that you have missed your direction, or seem uncertain of your destination, you should always look assertive; as if you are sure of where you are headed to. Do not hesitate to say No to any unsolicited help. Instead, walk into a nearby restaurant, hotel or government facility and ask for help.

Money robbers

Most of these money-robbers lurk around areas where ATMs are found. In some reported cases, there are scenarios where they kidnap their victims who have withdrawn money from such ATMs and force them back to withdraw more money from the same machines.

These Criminals are daring cowards who prefer to operate in secluded areas; areas where they are alone with their victims. To be safe from them, avoid secluded places. Significantly, it is advisable to withdraw money from banks and ATMs during daytime; when other clients are around. Or you should only access the local ATM's when you feel it's safe to do so.

The 'fare hike'

Some few unlicensed taxis in Rio de Janeiro are notorious for charging visitors excessive fares. If a taxi driver insists that you to pay the fare charge up-front, you should know that you are in for a 'hiked ride'.

 Many licensed taxis in Rio are fitted with taximeters. Any fare charge is supposed to be displayed on the vehicle's meter screen; the moment you reach your intended destination. The taximeters usefully convert the amount of time taken and distance traveled into fare charge. When you enter a taxi and the driver insists that you pay the fare charge up-front, the wisest thing you can do is to get out of such a taxi.

And in order to stay safe throughout your journey, avoid use of unlicensed taxis as sometimes, others have ended up robbing their innocent passengers. It's also advisable to pay the fare charge in the local currency so as to shield you from paying excess amounts linked to unclear exchange rates.

Pickpockets

Pickpockets usually take advantage of crowded or busy venues to 'silently' steal from their 'un-alert' victims. Mostly, they operate in groups and use distraction as a way of luring the attention of their victims. They may fake a very 'luring scene' and in the process, silently steal items placed in the open pockets of their victims.

Wallets, Jewelry, Watches, iPods, iPads, and Cell phones are some of the favorite items pickpockets are notorious for stealing. They prefer to operate around beaches, airports, and in any other venues where there is a sizeable group of people.

Author's Note/Acknowledgements

Writing any material about Brazil; the South American economic giant, has never been an easy assignment. The country is richly blessed with vast array of both natural and artificial resources.

The country's diverse flora and fauna is to date, unrivaled by any other country on the planet. And Brazilians are not only warm, but are welcoming, humble, playful and lovely.

Digging into the rich history, culture and geography of Brazil and to finally have this successful piece of information, is worthy of a celebration similar to the country's carnivals.

And in the same celebratory rejoinder, I am humbly indebted to the below offices, materials, resources, and websites, for their invaluable and in depth contribution towards making this noble assignment a reality.

The Brazilian Embassy in Kuwait, The Brazilian Embassy in Wellington, UNESCO, Brazil: The Home of Amazon (Rafara M), The Financial Times (UK), www.braziltravelinformation.com, www.brazil.org.za 2011, www.bahiatursa.ba.gov.br

With lots of sincerity, I equally, wish to thank every other person, who in one way or the other supported this work. I owe a lot of gratitude to God, the Almighty, for the gift of life, strength and resilience. And last but not least, I am humbled by the continued, unrelenting support, of my family members and close friends. It is through their prayers and physical support that this work has finally seen daylight.

Abbreviations

UNESCO	United Nations Educational, Scientific and Cultural Organization.
IBGE	Instituto Brasileiro de Geografia e Estatística (Brazilian Institute For Geography and Statistics).
FIFA	The Fédération Internationale de Football Association.
GDP	Gross Domestic Product.
ICCA	International Congress and Convention Association.
PPP	Purchasing Power Parity.
ATMs	Automated Teller Machines.
PHD	Doctor of Philosophy.
MD	Medical Doctor.
EST	Eastern Standard Time.
ANATEL	Agência Nacional de Telecomunicações (The National Telecommunications Agency).
GSM	Global System for Mobile Communications.
TDMA	Time Division Multiple Access.
AMPS	Advanced Mobile Phone System.
CDMA	Code division multiple access
WCDMA	Wideband Code Division Multiple Access.
LENT	A Christian season of preparation before Easter. Ash Wednesday usually marks its first day.
GCIH	The Order of Prince Henry the Navigator.
F	Fahrenheit (temperature Scale).
Kg	Kilograms (a metric measure of mass).
C	Celsius (Unit of measurement for Temperature).

Made in the USA
San Bernardino, CA
13 September 2016